JUICING RECIPE BOOK
for Cancer

A Comprehensive Guide to Healing
Your Body from the Inside Out:
Juicing for Cancer Prevention and
Treatment

Dr. Mariah Powell

Copyright © 2023 By Dr. Mariah Powell

Table of Contents

INTRODUCTION

" You could die in 2 years if proper care is not taken, you can start bidding farewell to your family." This was the story of a woman who was faced with a difficult battle. She had been diagnosed with cancer, and it seemed like an impossible challenge. She was scared, she was uncertain, and she felt like she had no control. But there was one thing she could do to fight back. She could take charge of her health, and she could use the power of nutrition to help her body heal.

With that in mind, she set out on a journey to learn more about the healing power of food and nutrition. She read books, watched documentaries, went to seminars, and she talked to experts. She was determined to find a way to fight her disease naturally, using the power of nutrition.

And that's when she came across the concept of juicing for cancer. She had heard of some people using juicing to boost their immune systems and fight off illnesses, but she had never heard of someone using it to fight cancer. But she was captivated by the idea, and she decided to give it a try.

So begins the story of "Juicing for Cancer," a book that dives deeply into the power of nutrition and how it can be used to fight cancer.

In this book, you will learn about the science behind juicing and how it can be used to give your body the nutrition it needs to fight off cancer cells. You will discover how to make delicious juice recipes that are tailored to your particular needs, and you will also gain insight into the psychological and emotional aspects of juicing for cancer.

This book is not just about juicing for cancer, it is about the journey of healing. It is about the power of nutrition and how it can be used to empower you to transform your life. It is about the courage it takes to fight an illness and the strength that comes when you trust in yourself and in the healing power of nutrition.

This book is for anyone who is facing a difficult battle with cancer, and for anyone who is interested in learning more about the healing power of nutrition. It is a powerful story of how juicing for cancer can be used to fight an illness and to create a healthier, happier, and more vibrant life. So if you are ready to take charge of your health and to make a change, then this book is for you.

CHAPTER 1: INTRODUCTION TO JUICING FOR CANCER

1:1 What is Cancer?

Cancer is a complex group of diseases that occurs when cells in the body divide and grow abnormally and uncontrollably.

This uncontrolled growth can spread throughout the body, invading other organs and tissues, and can become life-threatening.

Cancer is caused by a combination of environmental, genetic, and lifestyle factors, and is the second leading cause of death globally.

Although there are numerous types and subtypes of cancer, they all share the common characteristic of uncontrolled cell growth. Treatments and therapies can vary depending on the type and stage of cancer, but often include surgery, chemotherapy, radiation therapy, and immunotherapy.

Despite the devastating effects of cancer, advances in research and treatments have made great progress in the prevention, detection, and treatment of the disease, which has helped to prolong the quality of life for millions of people worldwide.

1:2 Juicing Basics

Juicing is a term used to describe the process of extracting juice from fruits and vegetables. This process can be done using a dedicated juicing machine or by using a blender and a strainer. Juicing is a popular way to get more of the vitamins, minerals, and other nutrients from fruits and vegetables into your diet. It also allows you to create delicious and nutritious drinks in a matter of minutes.

It helps to increase the intake of fruits and vegetables, which are full of essential vitamins, minerals, and antioxidants that can help to improve overall health and well-being. Juicing also allows for a variety of flavors and combinations to be created, as well as helping to make it easier to consume more nutritious foods in an enjoyable way.

1:3 Learn How To

1. Choose the right juicer - There are many different types of juicers available on the market, so it's important to choose one that meets your needs. Consider the type of ingredients you'll be juicing, how much space you have to store a juicer, and how much juice you'd like to make at once.

2. Prepare your produce - Wash and cut up all of your produce into smaller pieces for easier juicing.

3. Add your ingredients - Place the prepared fruits and vegetables into the juicer, one at a time. Make sure to alternate between hard and soft ingredients to help the juicer work more efficiently.

4. Extract the juice - Turn on the machine and let it do its job. Depending on the type of juicer you have, the process can take anywhere from a few seconds to several minutes.

5. Enjoy your juice - Pour the juice into glasses and add any additional ingredients, such as honey or lemon juice, for extra flavor. Enjoy your freshly made juice right away or store it in the refrigerator for later.

1:4 Benefits of Juicing for Cancer

1. Increased Nutrient Intake: Juicing provides cancer patients with a concentrated dose of essential vitamins, minerals, and other important nutrients that can help support the body's natural healing processes.

2. Improved Digestion: Juicing can help reduce the strain on the digestive system and provide a more easily-digestible source of nutrition for cancer patients who may be having trouble eating and digesting solid food.

3. Anti-Cancer Properties: Certain fruits and vegetables contain powerful antioxidants and other compounds which may help reduce the risk of cancer recurrence and spread.

4. Improved Immune System: Juicing can help boost the immune system and help the body fight off infections and other illnesses.

5. Reduced Fatigue: Juicing can provide cancer patients with an energy boost, helping them to feel less fatigued and better able to cope with their cancer treatments.

6. Stress Reduction: Juicing can help cancer patients relax and reduce stress levels, which can be beneficial for overall wellbeing.

7. Detoxification: Juicing helps to remove toxins from the body, which can be beneficial for cancer patients.

8. Improved Mood: Juicing can help improve a cancer patient's mood and reduce feelings of depression and anxiety.

9. Reduced Inflammation: Juicing can help reduce inflammation in the body, which can be beneficial for cancer patients.

10. Better Quality of Life: Juicing can help cancer patients feel better and enjoy a better quality of life.

11. Improved Appetite: Juicing can help cancer patients to better maintain a healthy appetite.

nausea associated with cancer treatments.

12. Improved Sleep: Juicing can help cancer patients to get better quality sleep.

13. Reduced Toxicity: Juicing can help reduce the toxicity of cancer treatments.

14. Alkalizing: Juicing can help to alkalize the body, which can be beneficial for cancer patients.

CHAPTER 2: GETTING STARTED

2:1 Starting Juicing for Cancer

1. Talk to your doctor about the safety and potential benefits of juicing for cancer.

2. Learn which fruits and vegetables are best for cancer-fighting properties.

3. Invest in a quality juicer that fits your budget and lifestyle.

4. Purchase organic produce whenever possible.

5. Wash your produce thoroughly.

6. Start out slowly with one or two juices per day.

7. Experiment with different combinations of fruits and vegetables to find the tastes you enjoy.

8. Drink your juice freshly made and within 20 minutes for maximum benefit.

9. Gradually increase your juice intake as your body adjusts.

10. Consider adding superfoods like turmeric, ginger, and wheatgrass to your juices.

11. Stay hydrated and ensure you are getting enough protein, fat, and carbohydrates in your diet.

12. Monitor your health and discuss any changes with your doctor.

2:2 Pros and Cons of Juicing for Cancer

Pros:

1. Juicing can provide a concentrated source of nutrients, vitamins, and minerals, which may help to improve overall health and well-being.

2. Juicing can help to reduce inflammation and oxidative stress, which are important factors in cancer prevention.

3. Juicing may help to boost the immune system, which could help the body fight off cancer.

4. Juicing can help to provide more energy and stamina, which may help the body to better cope with cancer treatments.

Cons:

1. Juicing can be expensive, depending on the type of juicer used and the ingredients chosen.

2. Juicing can require a lot of time and effort, and may not be feasible for everyone.

3. Juicing may not provide all the nutrients and vitamins that the body needs to fight cancer.

4. Juicing may not be suitable for certain types of cancer, such as pancreatic cancer, as certain fruits and vegetables can be too acidic.

2:3 Juicing Tips and Tricks

1. Use fresh, ripe produce.

2. Always wash and scrub your produce before juicing.

3. Use a combination of fruits and veggies for variety.

4. Start with sweeter fruits or veggies to make your juices more palatable.

5. Add a lemon or lime to your juice for a burst of flavor.

6. Use water or ice to thin out your juice if it's too thick.

7. Use a fine mesh strainer to strain out any pulp.

8. Drink your juice immediately after juicing for optimum nutritional benefits.

9. Experiment with different flavor combinations.

10. Use vegetable greens like spinach, kale, and chard for a nutrient-packed boost.

11. Add a scoop of your favorite protein powder for an extra protein punch.

12. Freeze extra juice for a cold, refreshing drink later.

13. Add a splash of honey or agave nectar for natural sweetness.

14. Try juicing with different herbs and spices for a unique flavor.

15. Start slowly to give your body time to adjust to the new juicing lifestyle.

16. Use a slow juicer for the most nutrient-packed juice.

17. Store your juice in a glass container to avoid plastic leaching into your juice.

18. Use green apples to add sweetness and tartness to your juice.

19. Avoid over-juicing certain fruits and vegetables like beets, carrots, and apples.

20. Drink plenty of water to help your body flush out the toxins released by juicing.

CHAPTER 3: HOW TO STORE FRESH JUICES

1. Refrigerate: Refrigerate freshly pressed juices immediately to slow the growth of bacteria that can cause spoilage.

2. Freeze: Juices can be frozen in an air-tight container for up to three months.

3. Can or bottle: Can or bottle juices in sterilized containers to preserve them for up to a year.

4. Dehydrate: Dehydrating juices concentrate on them and allow them to be stored for up to two years.

5. Make into popsicles: Freeze freshly pressed juices in popsicle molds for a healthy treat.

6. Store in the pantry: Unopened bottles of juices can be stored in the pantry for up to three months.

7. Use a vacuum sealer: Vacuum sealing juices helps them keep for up to two months.

8. Make ice cubes: Freeze freshly pressed juices in ice cube trays for quick additions to smoothies and other drinks.

9. Use a mason jar: Store freshly pressed juices in a mason jar for up to five days.

10. Add honey or lemon: Adding a natural preservative like honey or lemon juice can help extend the shelf life of freshly pressed juices.

CHAPTER 4: COLD-PRESSED JUICE

4:1 What is Cold-pressed Juice

Cold-pressed juice is a type of juice that is made by crushing and pressing fruits and vegetables without the use of heat. This type of juice is known for being richer in vitamins and minerals, as well as having a higher concentration of antioxidants. Cold-pressed juice is also known for being more flavorful and having a longer shelf life than juice made using traditional methods.

4:2 How to Cold-pressed Juice

1. Preparing the Equipment: Begin by cleaning and prepping your equipment, such as the juicer, containers, and any other tools you may need.

2. Prepping the Produce: Wash and prepare the produce for juicing. Trim off any bad spots, leaves, and

stems. Cut the produce into smaller pieces so they fit into the juicer.

3. Feed the Produce into the Juicer: Place the produce into the juicer and turn it on. Depending on the type of juicer you have, you may have to press the produce down or manually turn the handle.

4. Collect the Juice: As the juicer runs, the juice will start to be collected in a container. Be sure to keep an eye on the container as it will fill up quickly. Once it is full, turn off the juicer and pour the juice into a new container.

5. Clean the Juicer: Clean the juicer and all other tools used immediately after juicing. This will help prevent the buildup of bacteria and other contaminants.

6. Enjoy the Juice: Pour the juice into a glass or container and enjoy! Store any leftover juice in an airtight container in the refrigerator for up to three days.

4:3 The Benefits of Cold-Pressed Juice

1. Increased nutrient absorption: Cold-pressed juice contains more vitamins, minerals, and enzymes than other forms of juice, allowing for more efficient absorption of the beneficial nutrients.

2. Ease of digestion: Cold-pressed juice is easier on the digestive system, helping to reduce bloating and discomfort.

3. Increased energy: The combination of vitamins, minerals, and enzymes can help boost your energy levels.

4. Improved skin health: Cold-pressed juice is rich in antioxidants, which can help protect your skin from environmental damage and premature aging.

5. Detoxification: Cold-pressed juice helps to cleanse and detoxify the body by flushing out toxins.

6. Weight loss: Drinking cold-pressed juice can help you lose weight as it is low in calories and sugar.

7. Improved immunity: The nutrients in cold-pressed juice can help to strengthen your immune system and fight off illnesses.

8. Better hydration: Cold-pressed juice can help keep your body hydrated and energized, which can help improve your overall health.

9. Mental clarity: Cold-pressed juices are packed with vitamins and minerals that can help improve focus, concentration, and memory.

10. Boosted metabolism: Cold-pressed juice can help your body burn calories more efficiently, leading to increased weight loss.

CHAPTER 5: GUIDELINES FOR SAFE JUICING

1. Clean and sanitize all equipment before and after use.

2. Use only fresh fruits and vegetables that have been washed and dried.

3. Make sure you are using a juicer that is recommended by the manufacturer.

4. Do not add any additional ingredients such as sugar, salt, or artificial sweeteners.

5. Do not over-juice or blend as this can lead to nutrient loss.

6. Drink your juice right away and do not store it for future use.

7. Consume your juice within a few hours of making it.

8. If you have any health conditions, check with your doctor before juicing.

9. Do not feed juice to infants or children under the age of five.

10. Be aware of the benefits and possible side effects of the ingredients you are using.

CHAPTER 6: RECIPES FOR CANCER PREVENTION

6:1 Juicing Recipes for Cancer Prevention

Kale Delight

Blend 1 large kale leaf, 1 stalk of celery, 2 small apples, 1 inch of peeled ginger, 1/2 lemon, and 1/2 cup of water.

Pineapple Power

Blend 1 cup of pineapple, 1/2 cucumber, 1/2 lemon, 1/4 inch of peeled ginger, and 1/2 cup of water.

Green Warrior

Blend 1/2 cup of spinach, 1/2 cup of kale, 1/2 cup of cucumber, 1/2 cup of celery, 1/4 of lemon, 1/4 inch of peeled ginger, 1/2 cup of water, and 1/2 cup of ice.

Beet Booster

Blend 1/2 cup of cooked beets, 1/4 cup of carrots, 2

tablespoons of fresh parsley, 1/4 inch of peeled ginger, 1/4 of a lemon, and 1/2 cup of water.

Carrot Orange Splash

Blend 1/2 cup of carrots, 1/2 cup of orange juice, 1/4 inch of peeled ginger, 1/2 cup of water, and 1/2 cup of ice.

Apple Mint Refresher

Blend 1 cup of chopped apple, 1/4 cup of fresh mint leaves, 1/4 inch of peeled ginger, and 1/2 cup of water.

Carrot Citrus Blast

Blend 1 cup of chopped carrots, 1/2 cup of orange juice, 1/2 lemon, 1/4 inch of peeled ginger, and 1/2 cup of water.

Cucumber Celery Surprise

Blend 1/2 cup of cucumber, 1/2 cup of celery, 1/2 cup of spinach, 1/2 cup of water, and 1/2 cup of ice.

Beet Cucumber Blend

Blend 1/2 cup of cooked beets, 1/2 cup of cucumber,

1/4 cup of orange juice, 1/4 inch of peeled ginger, 1/4 of a lemon, and 1/2 cup of water.

Tomato Tango

Blend 1 cup of chopped tomato, 1/2 cup of celery, 1/2 cup of kale, 1/2 lemon, 1/4 inch of peeled ginger, and 1/2 cup of water.

Green Goddess

Blend 1/2 cup of spinach, 1/2 cup of kale, 1/4 cup of parsley, 1/4 cup of cucumber, 1/4 of lemon, 1/4 inch of peeled ginger, and 1/2 cup of water.

Mango Mint

Blend 1 cup of chopped mango, 1/4 cup of fresh mint leaves, 1/4 inch of peeled ginger, and 1/2 cup of water.

Carrot Apple Sweet

Blend 1 cup of chopped carrots, 1 cup of chopped apple, 1/4 inch of peeled ginger, 1/4 of a lemon, and 1/2 cup of water.

Orange Delight

Blend 1/2 cup of orange juice, 1/2 cup of cucumber, 1/4 cup of chopped spinach, 1/4 inch of peeled ginger, and 1/2 cup of water.

Blueberry Booster

Blend 1 cup of blueberries, 1/2 cup of spinach, 1/4 inch of peeled ginger, 1/4 of a lemon, and 1/2 cup of water.

Carrot Melon Splash

Blend 1/2 cup of carrots, 1/2 cup of cantaloupe, 1/4 cup of orange juice, 1/4 inch of peeled ginger, and 1/2 cup of water.

Strawberry Sipper

Blend 1 cup of chopped strawberries, 1/2 cup of kale, 1/4 inch of peeled ginger, 1/4 of a lemon, and 1/2 cup of water.

Green Machine

Blend 1/2 cup of spinach, 1/2 cup of kale, 1/2 cup of celery, 1/2 cup of cucumber, 1/4 inch of peeled ginger, 1/4 of lemon, and 1/2 cup of water.

Apple Cider

Blend 1 cup of chopped apples, 1/4 cup of fresh parsley, 1/4 cup of apple cider vinegar, 1/4 inch of peeled ginger, and 1/2 cup of water.

Pineapple Carrot

Blend 1/2 cup of pineapple, 1/2 cup of carrots, 1/4 cup of orange juice, 1/4 inch of peeled ginger, and 1/2 cup of water.

Beet Refresher

Blend 1/2 cup of cooked beets, 1/2 cup of spinach, 1/4 cup of orange juice, 1/4 inch of peeled ginger, 1/4 of a lemon, and 1/2 cup of water.

Spinach Apple

Blend 1/2 cup of spinach, 1/2 cup of chopped apples, 1/4 inch of peeled ginger, 1/4 of lemon, and 1/2 cup of water.

Berry Treat

Blend 1 cup of mixed berries, 1/2 cup of celery, 1/2 cup of cucumber, 1/4 inch of peeled ginger, and 1/2 cup of water.

Carrot Cucumber

Blend 1/2 cup of carrots, 1/2 cup of cucumber, 1/4 cup of orange juice, 1/4 inch of peeled ginger, and 1/2 cup of water.

Citrus Breeze

Blend 1/2 cup of orange juice, 1/2 cup of kale, 1/4 cup of cucumber, 1/4 inch of peeled ginger, 1/4 of a lemon, and 1/2 cup of water.

Carrot Mango

Blend 1/2 cup of carrots, 1/2 cup of chopped mango, 1/4 inch of peeled ginger, and 1/2 cup of water.

Green Delight

Blend 1/2 cup of spinach, 1/2 cup of kale, 1/2 cup of cucumber, 1/4 cup of orange juice, 1/4 inch of peeled ginger, and 1/2 cup of water.

Beet Berry

Blend 1/2 cup of cooked beets, 1/2 cup of mixed

berries, 1/4 cup of orange juice, 1/4 inch of peeled ginger, 1/4 of a lemon, and 1/2 cup of water.

Apple Celery

Blend 1 cup of chopped apples, 1/2 cup of celery, 1/4 inch of peeled ginger, 1/4 of a lemon, and 1/2 cup of water.

Carrot Orange

Blend 1/2 cup of carrots, 1/2 cup of orange juice, 1/4 inch of peeled ginger, and 1/2 cup of water.

Cucumber Lime

Blend 1/2 cup of cucumber, 1/4 cup of freshly squeezed lime juice, 1/4 inch of peeled ginger, and 1/2 cup of water.

Pineapple Spinach

Blend 1/2 cup of pineapple, 1/2 cup of spinach, 1/4 cup of orange juice, 1/4 inch of peeled ginger, and 1/2 cup of water.

Watermelon Sunrise

Blend 1/2 cup of diced watermelon, 1/4 cup of celery, 1/4 cup of orange juice, 1/4 inch of peeled ginger, and 1/2 cup of water.

Carrot Parsley

Blend 1/2 cup of carrots, 1/4 cup of fresh parsley, 1/4 inch of peeled ginger, 1/4 of a lemon, and 1/2 cup of water.

Mango Celery

Blend 1 cup of chopped mango, 1/2 cup of celery, 1/4 inch of peeled ginger, and 1/2 cup of water.

Grapefruit Refresher

Blend 1/2 cup of freshly squeezed grapefruit juice, 1/4 cup of celery, 1/4 cup of cucumber, 1/4 inch of peeled ginger, and 1/2 cup of water.

Apple Berry

Blend 1 cup of chopped apples, 1/2 cup of mixed berries, 1/4 inch of peeled ginger, 1/4 of a lemon, and 1/2 cup of water.

Pineapple Mint

Blend 1/2 cup of pineapple, 1/4 cup of fresh mint leaves, 1/4 inch of peeled ginger, and 1/2 cup of water.

Tomato Carrot

Blend 1 cup of chopped tomatoes, 1/2 cup of carrots, 1/4 inch of peeled ginger, 1/4 of a lemon, and 1/2 cup of water.

Tropical Breeze

Blend 1/2 cup of pineapple, 1/2 cup of mango, 1/4 cup of orange juice, 1/4 inch of peeled ginger, and 1/2 cup of water.

Kale Apple

Blend 1/2 cup of kale, 1 cup of chopped apples, 1/4 inch of peeled ginger, 1/4 of a lemon, and 1/2 cup of water.

Green Lemonade

Blend 1/2 cup of spinach, 1/2 cup of kale, 1/2 cup of cucumber, 1/4 cup of freshly squeezed lemon juice, 1/4 inch of peeled ginger, and 1/2 cup of water.

Carrot Melon

Blend 1/2 cup of carrots, 1/2 cup of diced melon, 1/4 cup of orange juice, 1/4 inch of peeled ginger, and 1/2 cup of water.

Cucumber Parsley

Blend 1/2 cup of cucumber, 1/4 cup of fresh parsley, 1/4 inch of peeled ginger, 1/4 of a lemon, and 1/2 cup of water.

Mango Spinach

Blend 1/2 cup of chopped mango, 1/2 cup of spinach, 1/4 cup of orange juice, 1/4 inch of peeled ginger, and 1/2 cup of water.

Carrot Cider

Blend 1/2 cup of carrots, 1/4 cup of apple cider vinegar, 1/4 inch of peeled ginger, 1/4 of a lemon, and 1/2 cup of water.

Raspberry

Sweet: Blend 1 cup of raspberries, 1/4 cup of carrots, 1/4 cup of orange juice, 1/4 inch of peeled ginger, and

1/2 cup of water.

Celery Lemon

Blend 1/2 cup of celery, 1/4 cup of freshly squeezed lemon juice, 1/4 inch of peeled ginger, and 1/2 cup of water.

Beet Berry Blast

Blend 1/2 cup of cooked beets, 1/2 cup of mixed berries, 1/4 cup of orange juice, 1/4 inch of peeled ginger, 1/4 of a lemon, and 1/2 cup of water.

Apple Parsley

Blend 1 cup of chopped apples, 1/4 cup of fresh parsley, 1/4 inch of peeled ginger, 1/4 of a lemon, and 1/2 cup of water.

CHAPTER 7: RECIPES FOR CANCER TREATMENT

7:1 Juicing Recipes for Cancer Treatment

Carrot, Apple, and Ginger Juice

Juice together 4 carrots, 1 apple, and a 1-inch piece of ginger for a nutritious anti-cancer juice.

Beet, Carrot, and Orange Juice

Juice together 1 beet, 2 carrots, and 1 orange for an anti-cancer juice rich in antioxidants.

Kale, Apple, and Lemon Juice

Juice together 2 cups of kale, 1 apple, and 1 lemon for an anti-cancer juice high in vitamins C and K.

Spinach, Apple, and Cucumber Juice

Juice together 1 cup of spinach, 1 apple, and 1 cucumber for a juice packed with cancer-fighting nutrients.

Celery, Parsley, and Lemon Juice

Juice together 1 stalk of celery, 1/4 cup of parsley, and 1 lemon for an anti-cancer juice.

Carrot, Beet, and Apple Juice

Juice together 2 carrots, 1 beet, and 1 apple for a juice full of cancer-fighting vitamins and minerals.

Cucumber, Kale, and Pineapple Juice

Juice together 1 cucumber, 1 cup of kale, and 1/2 cup of pineapple for a juice rich in cancer-fighting antioxidants.

Carrot, Apple, and Parsley Juice

Juice together 4 carrots, 1 apple, and 1/4 cup of parsley for a juice loaded with vitamins and minerals.

Beet, Carrot, and Spinach Juice

Juice together 1 beet, 2 carrots, and 1 cup of spinach for a juice full of cancer-fighting nutrients.

Carrot, Celery, and Ginger Juice

Juice together 4 carrots, 1 stalk of celery, and a 1-inch piece of ginger for a juice packed with antioxidants.

Beet, Apple, and Parsley Juice

Juice together 1 beet, 1 apple, and 1/4 cup of parsley for a juice high in cancer-fighting vitamins and minerals.

Kale, Carrot, and Orange Juice

Juice together 2 cups of kale, 2 carrots, and 1 orange for an anti-cancer juice.

Spinach, Apple, and Lemon Juice

Juice together 1 cup of spinach, 1 apple, and 1 lemon for a juice rich in cancer-fighting nutrients.

Carrot, Beet, and Cucumber Juice

Juice together 2 carrots, 1 beet, and 1 cucumber for a juice full of antioxidants.

Celery, Apple, and Parsley Juice

Juice together 1 stalk of celery, 1 apple, and 1/4 cup of parsley for a cancer-fighting juice.

Carrot, Parsley, and Ginger Juice

Juice together 4 carrots, 1/4 cup of parsley, and a 1-inch piece of ginger for a juice packed with vitamins and minerals.

Kale, Apple, and Cucumber Juice

Juice together 2 cups of kale, 1 apple, and 1 cucumber for a juice high in cancer-fighting nutrients.

Beet, Carrot, and Spinach Juice

Juice together 1 beet, 2 carrots, and 1 cup of spinach for a juice full of antioxidants.

Carrot, Celery, and Orange Juice

Juice together 4 carrots, 1 stalk of celery, and 1 orange for a cancer-fighting juice.

Spinach, Kale, and Pineapple Juice

Juice together 1 cup of spinach, 2 cups of kale, and 1/2 cup of pineapple for an anti-cancer juice.

Carrot, Apple, and Lemon Juice

Juice together 4 carrots, 1 apple, and 1 lemon for a juice full of vitamins and minerals.

Beet, Cucumber, and Parsley Juice

Juice together 1 beet, 1 cucumber, and 1/4 cup of parsley for a juice rich in cancer-fighting nutrients.

Carrot, Beet, and Orange Juice

Juice together 2 carrots, 1 beet, and 1 orange for a juice packed with cancer-fighting antioxidants.

Celery, Apple, and Ginger Juice

Juice together 1 stalk of celery, 1 apple, and a 1-inch piece of ginger for an anti-cancer juice.

Kale, Carrot, and Parsley Juice

Juice together 2 cups of kale, 2 carrots, and 1/4 cup of parsley for a juice high in vitamins and minerals.

Spinach, Apple, and Cucumber Juice

Juice together 1 cup of spinach, 1 apple, and 1 cucumber for a juice full of cancer-fighting nutrients.

Beet, Carrot, and Lemon Juice

Juice together 1 beet, 2 carrots, and 1 lemon for a juice rich in antioxidants.

Carrot, Celery, and Pineapple Juice

Juice together 4 carrots, 1 stalk of celery, and 1/2 cup of pineapple for a juice packed with cancer-fighting vitamins and minerals.

Kale, Beet, and Apple Juice

Juice together 2 cups of kale, 1 beet, and 1 apple for an anti-cancer juice.

Spinach, Cucumber, and Parsley Juice

Juice together 1 cup of spinach, 1 cucumber, and 1/4 cup of parsley for a juice high in cancer-fighting nutrients.

Carrot, Orange, and Ginger Juice

Juice together 4 carrots, 1 orange, and a 1-inch piece of ginger for a juice full of antioxidants.

Beet, Apple, and Cucumber Juice

Juice together 1 beet, 1 apple, and 1 cucumber for a juice packed with cancer-fighting vitamins and minerals.

Celery, Kale, and Lemon Juice

Juice together 1 stalk of celery, 2 cups of kale, and 1 lemon for an anti-cancer juice.

Carrot, Parsley, and Orange Juice

Juice together 4 carrots, 1/4 cup of parsley, and 1 orange for a juice rich in cancer-fighting nutrients.

Kale, Beet, and Spinach Juice

Juice together 2 cups of kale, 1 beet, and 1 cup of spinach for a juice full of antioxidants.

Carrot, Apple, and Cucumber Juice

Juice together 4 carrots, 1 apple, and 1 cucumber for a juice packed with vitamins and minerals.

Beet, Celery, and Parsley Juice

Juice together 1 beet, 1 stalk of celery, and 1/4 cup of parsley for a cancer-fighting juice.

Spinach, Orange, and Ginger Juice

Juice together 1 cup of spinach, 1 orange, and a 1-inch piece of ginger for a juice high in cancer-fighting nutrients.

Carrot, Kale, and Pineapple Juice

Juice together 4 carrots, 2 cups of kale, and 1/2 cup of pineapple for an anti-cancer juice.

Beet, Apple, and Lemon Juice

Juice together 1 beet, 1 apple, and 1 lemon for a juice full of antioxidants.

Celery, Carrot, and Parsley Juice

Juice together 1 stalk of celery, 2 carrots, and 1/4 cup of parsley for a juice rich in cancer-fighting vitamins and minerals.

Kale, Cucumber, and Orange Juice

Juice together 2 cups of kale, 1 cucumber, and 1 orange for a juice packed with cancer-fighting nutrients.

Spinach, Apple, and Ginger Juice

Juice together 1 cup of spinach, 1 apple, and a 1-inch piece of ginger for an anti-cancer juice.

Carrot, Beet, and Pineapple Juice

Juice together 2 carrots, 1 beet, and 1/2 cup of pineapple for a juice full of vitamins and minerals.

Celery, Parsley, and Lemon Juice

Juice together 1 stalk of celery, 1/4 cup of parsley, and 1 lemon for a juice high in cancer-fighting antioxidants.

Kale, Carrot, and Cucumber Juice

Juice together 2 cups of kale, 2 carrots, and 1 cucumber for a juice packed with cancer-fighting nutrients.

Beet, Spinach, and Apple Juice

Juice together 1 beet, 1 cup of spinach, and 1 apple for a juice rich in antioxidants.

Carrot, Orange, and Parsley Juice

Juice together 4 carrots, 1 orange, and 1/4 cup of parsley for a juice full of cancer-fighting vitamins and minerals.

Celery, Kale, and Ginger Juice

Juice together 1 stalk of celery, 2 cups of kale, and a 1-inch piece of ginger for an anti-cancer juice.

Spinach, Beet, and Pineapple Juice

Juice together 1 cup of spinach, 1 beet, and 1/2 cup of pineapple for a juice packed with cancer-fighting nutrients.

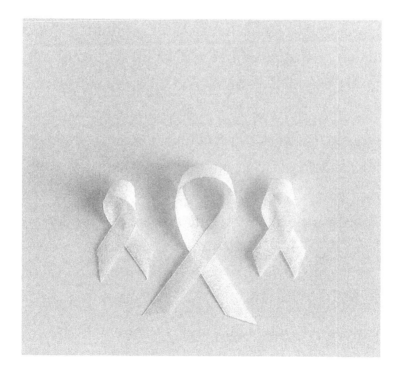

CHAPTER 8: THE ROLE OF ANTIOXIDANTS IN CANCER PREVENTION

Antioxidants are substances that help protect cells from the damage caused by unstable molecules known as free radicals. Free radicals are produced as a by-product of normal metabolism, but they can also be caused by exposure to environmental toxins, such as cigarette smoke, radiation, and air pollution.

The accumulation of free radical damage can lead to the development of cancer, as well as other diseases.

Antioxidants work by providing an electron to the free radical molecule, thus neutralizing it and preventing it from attacking healthy cells. By neutralizing free radicals, antioxidants help to prevent cellular damage, which can in turn reduce the risk of cancer.

In addition to helping to prevent cancer, antioxidants may also play a role in cancer treatment. Studies have shown that antioxidants may help to reduce the side effects of chemotherapy and radiation therapy. Antioxidants may also help to reduce inflammation, which can be beneficial for people with cancer.

Finally, antioxidants may help to reduce the risk of cancer recurrence. Studies have suggested that antioxidants may help to reduce the risk of cancer cells from recurring, thus helping to improve survival rates.

Overall, antioxidants play an important role in cancer prevention and treatment. By neutralizing free radicals and reducing inflammation, they can help to reduce the risk of cancer and improve survival rates in those who have had cancer. Additionally, antioxidants may help to reduce the side effects of chemotherapy and radiation therapy.

CHAPTER 9: THE ROLE OF VITAMINS AND MINERALS IN CANCER PREVENTION

1. Vitamin A: helps protect against cancer by maintaining healthy cells and controlling cell death

2. Vitamin B1: helps to create energy in the body and can help reduce the risk of certain cancers

3. Vitamin B2: helps protect against damage caused by free radicals and can help reduce the risk of certain types of cancer

4. Vitamin B3: helps to increase the immune system, which can help reduce the risk of cancer

5. Vitamin B6: helps to regulate certain hormones which can help reduce the risk of certain cancers

6. Vitamin B9: helps to regulate cell growth and can help reduce the risk of certain cancers

7. Vitamin B12: helps to create energy in the body and can help reduce the risk of certain cancers

8. Vitamin C: helps to protect against damage caused by free radicals and can help reduce the risk of certain types of cancer

9. Vitamin D: helps to regulate cell growth and can help reduce the risk of certain cancers

10. Vitamin E: helps to protect against damage caused by free radicals and can help reduce the risk of certain types of cancer

11. Vitamin K: helps to regulate cell growth and can help reduce the risk of certain cancers

12. Magnesium: helps to regulate cell growth and can help reduce the risk of certain cancers

13. Zinc: helps to regulate cell growth and can help reduce the risk of certain cancers

14. Selenium: helps to protect against damage caused by free radicals and can help reduce the risk of certain types of cancer

15. Copper: helps to create energy in the body and can help reduce the risk of certain cancers

16. Manganese: helps to regulate cell growth and can help reduce the risk of certain cancers

17. Chromium: helps to regulate cell growth and can help reduce the risk of certain cancers

18. Molybdenum: helps to create energy in the body and can help reduce the risk of certain cancers

19. Iron: helps to regulate cell growth and can help reduce the risk of certain cancers

20. Iodine: helps to regulate cell growth and can help reduce the risk of certain cancers

CHAPTER 10: THE ROLE OF FIBER IN CANCER PREVENTION

1. Fiber helps to reduce the risk of colorectal cancer by increasing stool bulk and decreasing the transit time of food through the intestines.

2. Fiber binds to bile acids and helps to reduce their absorption and the risk of colonic cancer.

3. Fiber helps to reduce the availability of carcinogenic compounds by binding to them and preventing their absorption.

4. Fiber helps to reduce the risk of breast cancer by helping to reduce the levels of circulating estrogen in the body.

5. Fiber helps to reduce the risk of esophageal cancer by binding to carcinogenic compounds in food and preventing their absorption.

6. Fiber helps to reduce the risk of ovarian cancer by binding to carcinogenic compounds in food and preventing their absorption.

7. Fiber helps to reduce the risk of pancreatic cancer by helping to increase the speed of food through the intestines and reducing the amount of time carcinogenic compounds have to be in contact with the organs.

8. Fiber helps to reduce the risk of endometrial cancer by helping to reduce the levels of circulating estrogen in the body.

9. Fiber helps to reduce the risk of stomach cancer by binding to carcinogenic compounds in food and preventing their absorption.

10. Fiber helps to reduce the risk of prostate cancer by binding to carcinogenic compounds in food and preventing their absorption.

CHAPTER 11: NUTRITION AND CANCER

11:1 Nutritional Considerations for Cancer Patients

1. Increase intake of fresh fruits and vegetables, particularly dark green and yellow-orange vegetables, to maximize intake of vitamin A, vitamin C, and other antioxidants.

2. Consume a variety of protein sources, such as plant-based proteins, lean meats, and fish, to ensure an adequate intake of essential amino acids.

3. Include a variety of whole grains, such as oats, brown rice, quinoa, and barley, to provide essential vitamins, minerals, and fiber.

4. Avoid processed foods and high-fat foods, which can increase inflammation and reduce nutrient absorption.

5. Limit alcohol consumption, as alcohol may increase oxidative stress and reduce the effectiveness of chemotherapy.

6. Drink plenty of water to stay hydrated and support the body's natural detoxification processes.

7. Increase intake of omega-3 fatty acids, found in fish and other sources, to reduce inflammation and support immune health.

8. Consider taking a multivitamin and mineral supplement to ensure adequate intake of essential micronutrients.

9. Take extra care to avoid foodborne pathogens and food-drug interactions, as cancer treatment can weaken the body's ability to fight off infections.

10. Work with a registered dietitian or nutritionist to create an individualized nutrition plan that meets your specific needs.

11.2 Nutritional Needs for Cancer Patients

1. High-fiber foods: Eating a diet high in fiber can help reduce the risk of some types of cancer, including colon cancer. Whole grains, fruits, vegetables, and legumes are all good sources of fiber.

2. Antioxidant-rich foods: Eating foods that are rich in antioxidants, such as berries and other brightly colored fruits and vegetables, can help reduce inflammation and protect cells from damage

3. Healthy fats: Healthy fats, such as those found in olive oil, avocados, and nuts, can help reduce inflammation and support the immune system.

4. Plant-based proteins: Plant-based proteins, such as beans, lentils, and quinoa, can provide essential nutrients and help reduce inflammation.

5. Vitamin-rich foods: Eating foods that are rich in vitamins, such as dark leafy greens, citrus fruits, and bell peppers, can help protect the body from free radicals and support the immune system.

6. Fermented foods: Fermented foods, such as sauerkraut and kimchi, can provide beneficial bacteria that can help support the immune system.

7. Hydrating fluids: Drinking plenty of fluids, such as water, herbal teas, and vegetable juices, can help keep the body hydrated and reduce inflammation.

11:3 Diet and Exercise Recommendations

Diet:

• Eat a balanced and varied diet that includes plenty of fruits and vegetables.

• Choose whole grains instead of processed grains.

• Limit your intake of red and processed meats.

• Avoid sugary drinks and instead opt for water, tea, or other low-calorie beverages.

• Limit your intake of saturated and trans fats.

• Include healthy sources of protein such as fish, chicken, beans, and nuts.

• Choose healthy fats such as olive oil, avocados, and nuts.

Exercise:

• Slowly incorporate physical activity into your daily routine.

• Aim for at least 30 minutes of moderate-intensity physical activity, such as walking, every day.

• If you are able, increase the intensity of your activity to include strength training and aerobic exercise.

• Work with your healthcare team to find the right activity for you.

• Be sure to stay hydrated and rest when needed.

CHAPTER 12: OTHER NATURAL THERAPIES FOR CANCER

12.1 Botanical Medicine

1. Echinacea (Echinacea angustifolia) - used for its immune-stimulating, antiviral, anti-inflammatory, and antitumor effects

2. Burdock Root (Arctium lappa) - used for its detoxification, antioxidant, and anti-cancer properties

3. Astragalus Root (Astragalus membranaceus) - used for its immunomodulating, anti-inflammatory, and antioxidant effects

4. Milk Thistle (Silybum marianum) - used for its liver-protective and anti-cancer effects

5. Elderberry (Sambucus nigra) - used for its antiviral, anti-inflammatory, and antioxidant properties

6. Reishi Mushroom (Ganoderma lucidum) - used for its immunomodulating, anti-inflammatory, and anti-cancer effects

7. Turmeric (Curcuma longa) - used for its anti-inflammatory and antioxidant effects

8. Ginger (Zingiber officinale) - used for its anti-inflammatory, antioxidant, and anticancer effects

9. Garlic (Allium sativum) - used for its antimicrobial, antiviral, and anticancer properties

10. Green Tea (Camellia sinensis) - used for its antioxidant, anti-inflammatory, and anticancer effects

12.2 Mind-Body Medicine

1. Meditation and Breathing Exercises: Regular practice of meditation and controlled breathing techniques can help reduce stress and anxiety associated with cancer treatment, boost immunity, and help alleviate symptoms such as pain, fatigue, and nausea.

2. Visualization: Visualization can be a powerful tool for cancer patients. Imagining positive outcomes and visualizing the body's ability to heal can help reduce fear and worry, and can even help to stimulate the body's natural healing abilities.

3. Exercise: Exercise can help to keep the body strong and boost immunity. Regular exercise can also help reduce fatigue, improve mood, and reduce stress and anxiety.

4. Healthy Diet: Eating healthy, nutrient-rich foods, such as fruits and vegetables, can help boost the body's natural defenses and provide important vitamins and minerals.

5. Aromatherapy: Essential oils can be used to reduce stress and anxiety, alleviate pain and nausea, and improve mood.

6. Acupuncture: Acupuncture can help reduce pain and nausea, improve energy levels, and reduce anxiety and depression.

7. Reiki: Reiki is a gentle, non-invasive form of energy healing that can help reduce stress and anxiety, and improve overall well-being.

8. Yoga: Yoga is an excellent way to reduce stress and anxiety, improve flexibility, and improve overall physical and mental health.

12.3 Homeopathy

Homeopathy is a form of alternative medicine that uses natural substances to promote healing and strengthen the body's own healing processes. Homeopathy is based on the belief that "like cures like" and utilizes small doses of natural substances that are believed to cause similar symptoms of the disease or condition being treated. Homeopathy for cancer involves using natural substances such as herbs and minerals to help reduce inflammation, boost the immune system, and target malignant cells. Homeopathic remedies can also be used to help relieve symptoms associated with cancer such as pain, nausea, and fatigue. Research suggests that homeopathic remedies may be beneficial in the treatment of certain types of cancer, although more studies are needed to confirm this. When considering homeopathic treatments for cancer, it is important to seek advice from a qualified homeopath.

Samples:

1. Acidum Phosphoricum 30C: This remedy can be used to help treat cancer of the stomach, intestines, pancreas, and other organs.

2. Carcinosinum 30C: This remedy is often used to help treat cancer of the breast, prostate, and other organs.

3. Conium Maculatum 30C: This remedy is often used to help treat cancer of the liver and other organs.

4. Natrum Muriaticum 30C: This remedy is often used to help treat cancer of the uterus, ovaries, and other organs.

5. Phosphorus 30C: This remedy is often used to help treat cancer of the lungs, liver, and other organs.

6. Thuja Occidentalis 30C: This remedy is often used to help treat cancer of the lymph nodes, skin, and other organs.

7. Aurum Metallicum 30C: This remedy is often used to help treat cancer of the bone, blood, and other organs.

CHAPTER 13: CONCLUSION

The journey to healing through juicing is long and difficult, but it doesn't have to be a lonely one. With the right resources, knowledge, and support, it can be a journey of discovery, renewal, and hope. Juicing for Cancer offers an invaluable resource to help you along the way.

13.1 From Me to You

I know your struggle,

I care for you deeply

in this difficult struggle.

I feel your sadness,

I know your fear,

I can only imagine

the worry and tears.

I can't take away your pain,

I can't make it go away,

but I will be with you,

each and every day.

I will be your strength,

I will be your guide,

I will be your comfort,

on this difficult ride.

I won't give up on you,

I won't ever leave,

I will stand by you

through this difficult time.

That is why I am putting my mail here to walk this journey with you. Send me a mail on anything that is bothering you and I am ready to walk with you toward your healing and recovery. I am here to provide you with the best possible support and guidance during this journey.

Mariahpowellcare@gmail.com

Printed in Great Britain
by Amazon

18498058R00047